You Can Make A Change

I0449356

You Can Make A Change

Delores Patterson

To order additional copies, please contact us.
BookSurge, LLC
www.booksurge.com
1-866-308-6235
orders@booksurge.com

You Can Make A Change

Introduction

There are many reasons why most Christians aren't living successful lives. Christians attend church, pray, read the Bible, give offerings, and pay tithe, but too often they experience failure and defeat in their daily lives. Many Christians have asked the question, "Why?" I believe that one of the reasons for this is that they haven't made changes in some important areas of their lives.

Most Christians will say that they have made a change when they received Christ as their personal savior. They will quote II Corinthians 5:17 which says, "Therefore if any man be in Christ, he is a new creature: old things are passed away; behold, all things are become new."

It is true that once you become born again that you are a new creature. You are a specie of being that has never previously existed. The part that says "All things are become new" is talking about your new spirit.

The minute you became a born again Christian, the spirit of Satan was ripped out of your spirit. God gave you a new spirit by putting His Spirit into your spirit.

Man is a tripartite being which means he is three part: spirit, soul, and body. Man is a spirit, he possesses a soul, and lives inside of a body.

When you became born again your mind and body did not undergo change, but your spirit did. You must present your body to God and renew your mind with the Word of God.

Romans 12:1,2 says, "I beseech you therefore brethren by the mercies of God, that ye present your bodies a living sacrifice, holy, acceptable unto God, which is your reasonable service. And be not conformed to this world: but be ye transformed by the renewing of your mind, that ye may prove what is that good, and acceptable, and perfect will of God."

God changed your spirit through the new birth. You are responsible for presenting your body to God and renewing your mind.

As one can see, making a change involves more than just giving your life to Christ. In this book entitled "You Can Make A Change", I will discuss two very important things that Christians must change so that they can experience success in every area of their lives.

Change the Way You Talk

Are you where you want to be at this time in your life? Have you accomplished all of your dreams or goals? Are you prospering financially, physically, spiritually, emotionally, and socially? If "No!" is your answer, I may have the solution for you. "Change the Way You Talk!" Changing the way you talk could change your life forever.

You must be convinced that God wants you to prosper in every area of your life.

Third John 2 says, "Beloved, I wish above all things that thou mayest prosper and be in health even as thy soul prospereth." God wants us to prosper financially, physically, and spiritually.

Some Christians think that prosperity is just having a lot of money. Prosperity includes having money and other things such as spiritual growth, physical, mental, and emotional well- being, and wholesome relationships.

Some Christians don't know that it is the Will of God for them to prosper.

Genesis 39:1-3

1 And Joseph was brought down to Egypt; and Potiphar, an officer of Pharaoh, captain of the guard, an Egyptian, bought

him (Joseph) of the hands of the Ishmeelites, which had brought him down thither.

2 And the Lord was with Joseph; and he was a prosperous man; and he was in the house of his master the Egyptian.

3 And his master saw that the Lord was with him, and that the Lord made all that he did to prosper in his hand.

Psalms 35:27 says "Let them shout for joy, and be glad, that favour my righteous cause; yea, let them say continually, Let the Lord be magnified, which hath pleasure in the prosperity of his servant."

The Will of God and the Word of God are one in the same. If Christians don't know the Word of God, they won't know His Will. That is the reason why they don't know what to speak out of their mouths.

Christians can use the Word of God to speak to their mountain of debt, sickness, depression, loneliness, doubt or any other thing and experience change.

Mark 11:23 says, "For verily I say unto you, That whosoever shall say unto this mountain, Be thou removed, and be thou cast into the sea; and shall not doubt in his heart, but shall believe that those things which he saith shall come to pass; he shall have whatsoever he saith."

Renew Your Mind With the Word of God

When I became a born again Christian, I thought that my life in Christ would have been a flowery-bed-of-ease. I thought that all of my problems were solved. Instead, it seemed as if Satan and his demons were coming after me.

As a baby Christian, I did not know that the words I spoke determined my future. I thought that if I didn't curse or use foul language that good things would happen in my life, but they didn't.

Practically all of my life, I've talked negatively and I've hung around negative people. I was not aware that negative words brought negative results and that positive words brought positive results. I learned later in my Christian walk, that I had to get into the Word of God in order to know what I should say. Training myself to say the right thing was difficult because some habits aren't easy to break.

One day, I said in all sincerity that I loved a certain individual to death. Immediately, I was corrected by a Christian friend who said, "Say I love you to life." I was shocked because I had not realized until then that I had spoken words of death instead of life towards that individual.

You and I have said some things all of our lives because they sounded like the right things to say or because we heard other people say them. When I renewed my mind with the Word of God, I learned to say the right things.

If you renew your mind and practice saying what the Word of God says about you, your life will change tremendously.

Romans 12:2 says, "And be not conformed to this world: but be ye transformed by the renewing of your mind, that ye may prove what is that good, and acceptable, and perfect will of God."

To renew your mind, you must study and meditate on the Word of God. When I learned what the Word of God said about me and began to speak it out of my mouth, it wasn't long before circumstances started changing in my life.

Your Words Determine Your Future

Proverbs 18:21 says, "Death and life are in the power of the tongue: and they that love it shall eat the fruit thereof."

You can speak life or death based upon what you say out of your mouth. You will suffer the consequences of what you say out of your mouth. I don't care if you are just joking. You will be rewarded with what comes out of your mouth.

Some Christians have made the following statements:
1. "I don't have a dime to my name."
2. "I can't win for losing."
3. You are getting on my last nerve."
4. "You have to die with something."
5. "I'm perishing."
6. "I'm cooking a poor man's meal."
7. "I'm broke, busted, and disgusted."

Proverbs 18:20 says, "A man's belly shall be satisfied with the fruit of his mouth; and with the increase of his lips shall he be filled."

Proverbs 18:20 (Amplified) says "A man's moral self shall be filled with the fruit of his mouth, and with the consequences of his words he must be satisfied whether good or evil."

The kind of seeds you sow will determine your harvest. The words that you speak out of your mouth are seeds. Seeds produce after their kind. If you plant good seeds into the ground, you will reap a good harvest. If you plant bad seeds into the ground, you will reap a bad harvest. Your heart (spirit) is your spiritual ground. If you sow the Word of God into your heart, you are bound to reap a good harvest.

Galatians 6:7 says "Be not deceived: God is not mocked: for whatsoever a man soweth that shall he also reap."

Words Have Creative Power

When I was a child I would say, "Sticks and stones will break my bones, but words will never hurt me." I have learned that words can hurt me because words carry power. If someone calls me "stupid" long enough, I will begin to believe that I am "stupid".

Words spoken negatively or positively have creative power. God spoke this physical world into existence with the power of words. You can speak your world into existence with the power of words.

If you speak negative words, you will experience negative results. If you speak positive words, you will experience positive results. Don't speak anything negative about your health, your finances, your children, your spouse or any other thing.

If things in your life aren't going the way that you think they should, say what the Word of God says about your situation.

Romans 4:17b says, "And calleth those things that be not as though they were."

If you are poor, say "I'm rich." If you are sick, say "I'm healed." If you feel defeated, say "I have the victory." If you feel disturbed in your spirit, say "I have peace." Don't say it one time, but say it until it becomes a reality in your life.

Proverbs 6:2 says, "Thou art snared with the words of thy mouth, thou art taken with the words of thy mouth."

Proverbs 6:2 (Amplified) says, "You are snared with the words of your lips, you are caught by the speech of your mouth."

That is why you must change the way you talk. When you speak words of doubt and unbelief, the devil and his demons come for your words. When you speak the Word of God, his angels come for your words to carry them out.

Psalms 103:20 says "Bless the Lord, ye his angels that excel in strength, that do his commandments, hearkening unto the voice of his word."

Hebrews 1:14 says, "Are they not all ministering spirits, sent forth to minister for them who shall be heirs of salvation?"

Post Guard Over Your Heart

Proverbs 4: 20-23 says, "My son attend to my words; incline thine ear unto my sayings. Let them not depart from thine eyes: keep them in the midst of thine heart. For they are life unto those that find them, and health to all their flesh. Keep thine heart (spirit) with all diligence for out of it are the issues of life."

You must post guard over your heart (spirit). Guard what you see with your eyes, hear with your ears, and speak out of your mouth. The things that you allow to come into your heart will determine your life.

What do you have in your heart? The things that are in your heart will come out of your mouth.

Matthew 12:34 says, "For out of the abundance of the heart the mouth speaketh."

Your Words Can Save or Destroy Your Life

The woman who had an issue of blood twelve long years spoke faith filled words that saved her life.

Mark 5:25-34

25 And a certain woman, which had an issue of blood twelve years,

26 And had suffered many things of many physicians; and had spent all that she had, and was nothing bettered, but rather grew worse,

27 When she had heard of Jesus, came in the press behind, and touched his garment,

28 For she said, If I may touch but his clothes, I shall be whole.

29 And straightway the fountain of her blood was dried up; and she felt in her body that she was healed of that plague.

30 And Jesus, immediately knowing in himself that virtue had gone out of him, turned him about in the press, and said, Who touched my clothes?

31 And his disciples said unto him, Thou seest the multitude thronging thee, and sayest thou, Who touched me?

32 And he looked round about to see her that had done this thing.

33 But the woman fearing and trembling, knowing what was done to her, came and fell down before him, and told him all the truth.

34 And he said unto her, Daughter, thy faith hath made thee whole; go in peace, and be whole of thy plague.

This woman spoke the outcome, moved out by faith, and received her healing. The words that she spoke out of her mouth brought life instead of death.

Think about it. What have you been saying lately? What kind of results have you gotten?

This woman didn't say what she couldn't do; she said what she would do. Instead of saying what you can't do, say what you can do.

Philippians 4:13 says, "I can do all things through Christ which strengtheneth me."

When Christians walk in fear, it is a sign that they have more faith in the lies of Satan instead of having faith in the Word of God. All fear is bad and all fear comes from the devil. Fear is "false evidence appearing real." Fear can literally destroy your life.

For instance, Job's fears caused him to lose his possessions and his children. Job's fears opened a door for the devil to rob him.

Job 1:4,5 says "And his sons went and feasted in their houses, every one his day, and sent and called for their three sisters to eat and to drink with them. And it was so, when the days of their feasting were gone about, that Job sent and sanctified them, and rose up early in the morning, and offered burnt offering according to the number of them all: for Job said, It may be that my sons have sinned, and cursed God in their hearts. Thus did Job continually."

Job was operating in fear. Job 3:25 says, "For the thing which I greatly feared is come upon me, and that which I was afraid of is come unto me."

You should make this a faith confession concerning your children. "And all thy(my) children shall be taught of the Lord; and great shall be the peace of thy(my) children. In righteousness shalt thou be established: thou shalt be far from oppression; for thou shalt not fear: and from terror; for it shall not come near thee." Isaiah 54:13.14

There Are Several Things That Can Affect One's Speech:
1. What you allow to come through your eye and ear gates.
2. People that you fellowship with. (Ex. Church members, organizations, clubs, co-workers, family, friends).
3. Things that you open yourself up to. (Examples, movies, music, magazines, cults).
4. Your emotions.
5. Your circumstances/situations.
6. Fear.
7. Faith.
8. The Word of God.

The Word of God Should be in Your Mouth at All Times

Joshua 1:8 says, "This book of the law shall not depart out of thy mouth; but thou shalt meditate therein day and night, that thou mayest observe to do according to all that is written therein: for then thou shalt make thy way prosperous, and then thou shalt have good success."

This book of the law is the Word of God. If you don't meditate on the Word of God day and night, you won't have success naturally or spiritually.

You meditate by muttering, pondering, and thinking on the Word of God. As you speak the Word of God and obey it, you will experience success in every area of your life.

The Word of God Should Be in Your Mouth and in Your Heart

Romans 10:8 says, "But what saith it? The word is nigh thee, even in thy mouth, and in thy heart: that is, the word of faith, which we preach."

Words of Wealth Should be in Your Mouth and in Your Heart

Deuteronomy 8:18 says, "But thou shalt remember the Lord thy God: for it is he that giveth thee power to get wealth, that he may establish his covenant which he sware unto thy fathers, as it is this day."

Psalms 112:3 says, "Wealth and riches shall be in his house; and his righteousness endureth forever."

Psalms 66:12 says, "Thou hast caused men to ride over

our heads, we went through fire and through water: but thou broughtest us out into a wealthy place."

Proverbs 13:22 says, "A good man leaveth an inheritance to his children's children: and the wealth of the sinner is laid up for the just."

Words of Healing Should be in Your Mouth and in Your Heart

Exodus 15:26b says, "For I am the Lord that healeth thee."

Isaiah 53:5 says "But he was wounded for our transgressions, he was bruised for our iniquities: the chastisement of our peace was upon him; and with his stripes, we are healed."

Matthew 8:17 says, "That it might be fulfilled which was spoken by Isaiah the prophet, saying Himself took our infirmities, and bare our sicknesses."

I Peter 2:24 says, "Who his own self bare our sins in his own body on the tree, that we, being dead to sins, should live unto righteousness: by whose stripes ye were healed."

Words of Deliverance Should be in Your Mouth and in Your Heart

Job 5:19 says, "He shall deliver thee in six troubles: yea, in seven there shall no evil touch thee."

Psalms 56:13 says, "For thou hast delivered my soul from death: will not thou deliver my feet from falling, that I may walk before God in the light of the living."

Jeremiah 1:8 says, "Be not afraid of their faces: for I am with thee to deliver thee, saith the Lord."

2 Timothy 4:18 says, "And the Lord shall deliver me from every evil work, and will preserve me unto his heavenly kingdom: to whom be glory forever and ever. Amen."

Words of Salvation Should be in Your Mouth and in Your Heart

Romans 10:9,10 says, "That if thou shalt confess with thy mouth the Lord Jesus, and shalt believe in thine heart that God hath raised him from the dead, thou shalt be saved. For with the heart man believeth unto righteousness, and with the mouth confession is made unto salvation."

Acts 4:12 says, "Neither is there salvation in any other; for there is none other name under heaven given among men, whereby we must be saved."

Romans 1:16 says, "For I am not ashamed of the gospel of Christ: for it is the power of God unto salvation to every-one that believeth: to the Jew first, and also to the Greek."

Ephesians 2:8 says, "For by grace are ye saved through faith; and that not of yourselves: it is the gift of God."

Words of Peace Should be in Your Mouth and in Your Heart

Psalms 29:11 says, "The Lord will give strength unto his people; the Lord will bless his people with peace."

Isaiah 26:3 says, "Thou wilt keep him in perfect peace, whose mind is stayed on thee: because he trusteth in thee."

Philippians 4:7 says, "And the peace of God, which passeth all understanding, shall keep your hearts and minds through Christ Jesus."

Colossians 3:15 says, "And let the peace of God rule in your hearts, to the which also ye are called in one body; and be ye thankful."

Words of Victory Should be in Your Mouth and in Your Heart

I Corinthians 15:57 says, "But thanks be to God , which giveth us the victory through our Lord Jesus Christ."

I John 5:4 says, "For whosoever is born of God overcometh the world: and this is the victory that overcometh the world, even our faith."

2 Corinthians 2:14 says, "Now thanks be unto God, which always causeth us to triumph in Christ, and maketh manifest the savor of his knowledge by us in every place."

Romans 8:37 says, "Nay, in all these things we are more than conquerors through him that loved us."

Change the Way You Think

C hanging the way you think is as equally important as changing the way you talk. What kinds of thoughts have you allowed to run through your mind? What do you think about the most? Do you think that you will never amount to anything? Do you think that you will never get out of debt? Do you think that you will never own the dream house or car that you want? Do you think that you will never get healed? Do you think that you will never own your own business? Do you think that your life has no meaning or purpose? If "yes" is your answer, I may have the solution for you. "Change the Way You Think!" Changing the way you think could change your life forever.

What you believe has a lot to do with how you think. Thoughts come from two places: from God and from Satan. Satan will fill your mind with evil thoughts if you allow him to. God will fill your mind with good thoughts. You will have to decide who you will submit your mind to. You will either submit your mind to God or to Satan.

James 4:7 says, "Submit yourselves therefore to God. Resist the devil, and he will flee from you." You can resist the devil by submitting to or obeying the Word of God.

Romans 6:16 says, "Know ye not that to whom ye yeild yourselves to obey, his servant ye are to whom ye obey.

Whether of sin unto death, or obedience unto righteousness?"

Satan's goal is to control your mind through lies and deceptions. He will tell you that God won't keep his Word. God is a covenant-keeping God.

It is impossible for God to lie. Numbers 23:19 says, "God is not a man, that he should lie; neither the son of man, that he should repent: hath he said, and shall he not do it? or hath he spoken, and shall he not make it good?"

Mark 13:31 says, "Heaven and earth shall pass away: but my words shall not pass away."

John 10:10 says, "The thief (Satan) cometh not, but for to steal, and to kill, and to destroy: I am come that they might have life, and that they might have it more abundantly."

John 8:44b says, "When he (Satan) speaketh a lie, he speaketh of his own: for he is a liar, and the father of it."

There Are Several Things That Can Affect How One Thinks:
1. Your family (beliefs).
2. Your friends/co-workers
3. Organizations/Clubs.
4. Things you have read or heard. (Ex. books, magazines, television, etc.).
5. Experiences.
6. Your church.
7. The devil.
8. The Word of God.

If Your Thinking is Wrong, Your Believing Will Be Wrong

Proverbs 23:7 says, "For as he thinketh in his heart, so is he." Who you think you are, is who you will become.

Ask yourself, "How can I change the way I think?" The Word of God tells you how.

Philippians 4:8 says, "Finally, brethren whatsoever things are true, whatsoever things are honest, whatsoever things are just, whatsoever things are pure, whatsoever things are lovely, whatsoever things are of good report; if there be any virtue, and if there be any praise think on these things."

True means genuine or real. Honest means to be free from fraud or deception. Just means right. Pure means free from contamination. Lovely means beautiful. A Good Report is an honest report. Virtue means moral excellence. Praise means worthy or commendable.

God wants you to think about things that are true, honest, just, pure, lovely, and of a good report. If you think on these things, you won't have any room in your mind to think about anything else.

Refuse to Believe Fables and Old Wives' Tales

Some people believe things that were passed down by their relatives. Some people have said to me, "That's what my grandma used to say." I know that they love their grandma, but grandma could be wrong.

I Timothy 1:4 says, "Neither give heed to fables and endless genealogies, which minister questions, rather than godly edifying which is in faith: so do."

I Timothy 4:7 says, "But refuse profane and old wives' fables and exercise thyself rather unto godliness."

Don't allow yourself to be drawn into arguments, quarrels, or debates with people over questions that are designed to turn you away from the uncompromising Word of God.

II Peters 2:1,2 says But there are false prophets also among the people, even as there shall be false teachers among you, who privily shall bring in damnable heresies, even denying the Lord that bought them, and bring upon themselves swift destruction. And many shall follow their pernicious ways; by reason of whom the way of truth shall be evil spoken of."

I Timothy 4:1 says, Now the Spirit speaketh expressively, that in the latter times some shall depart from the faith, giving heed to seducing spirits, and doctrines of devils."

What Does One Do With Thoughts That Are Contrary to the Word of God?

II Corinthians 10:4,5 says, "For the weapons of our warfare are not carnal, but mighty through God to the pulling down of strongholds. Casting down imaginations and every high thing that exalteth itself against the knowledge of God, and bringing into captivity every thought to the obedience of Christ."

Spiritual battles are won or lost in the mind. The mind is a spiritual battlefield. Satan fights us through our minds.

That's why we should cast down Satan's lies. We should cast down every thought that is not in line with the Word of God.

If we neglect to cast down evil thoughts that come from Satan, he will control our minds. That's why it is very important that we renew our minds with the Word of God. Renewing our minds with the Word of God will keep Satan from developing strongholds in our minds.

You should cast down:
1. Thoughts that say you will always be poor.
2. Thoughts that say God won't heal you.
3. Thoughts that say you are defeated.
4. Thoughts that say you are not going to make it.
5. Thoughts that say that you will never amount to anything.
6. Thoughts that say God doesn't love you.
7. Thoughts of fear.
8. Thoughts of worry.

I want to talk to you about "worry". Worry begins with a thought or an imagination. To worry is a sin because it causes you to doubt that God's Word is true. The Word of God says that we should never worry about anything. Most people find that hard to believe.

Matthew 6:25-26, 30-31 says, "Therefore I say unto you, Take no thought for your life, what ye shall eat, or what ye shall drink; nor yet for your body, what ye shall put on. Is not the life more than meat, and the body than raiment? Behold the fowls of the air: for they sow not, neither do they reap, nor gather into barns; yet your heavenly Father feedeth them. Are ye not much better than they? Wherefore, if God so clothe the grass of the field, which today is, and tomorrow is cast into the oven, shall he not much more clothe you, O ye of little faith? Therefore (don't worry) take no thought saying, What shall we eat? or, What shall we drink? or, Where withal shall we be clothed?"

The Word of God tells us to cast our cares on Jesus, when thoughts of worry come to our minds.

I Peter 5:7 says, "Casting all your care upon him; for he careth for you."

I Peter 5:7 (Amplified) says, "Casting the whole of your care-all your anxieties, all your worries, all your concerns, once and for all on Him (Jesus); for He cares for you affectionately, and cares about you watchfully."

Psalms 55:22 (Amplified) says, "Cast your burden on the Lord (releasing the weight of it) and He will sustain you. He will never allow the (consistently) righteous to be moved (made to slip, fall, or fail)."

The word "cast" means to send forth by throwing. Throw the whole of your anxieties, worries, and concerns once and for all on Jesus. Don't ever pick them up again and don't ever think about them.

Philippians 4:6 says, "Be careful for nothing (don't worry about anything); but in every thing by prayer and supplication with thanksgiving let your requests be made known unto God. And the peace of God, which passeth all understanding, shall keep your hearts and minds through Christ Jesus."

The Same Thoughts That God Has Towards Us Are the Same Thoughts That We Should Have Towards Ourselves

Genesis 1:31a, says, "And God saw everything that he made and behold, it was very good."

When God said that everything that he made was very good, that included you and me. You might say to yourself, "How could God be talking about you and me?"

Adam was the first man that God created. We were in the loins of Adam when God created him. In the mind of God, we already existed.

God not only called us very good, He created us unto good works.

Ephesians 2:10 says, "For we are his workmanship (masterpiece), created unto good works, which God hath before ordained that we should walk in them."

We Are Always on God's Mind and in His Thoughts

Hebrews 2:6a says, "But one in a certain place testified, saying what is man that thou art mindful of him?"

Psalms 115: 12-15 says, "The Lord hath been mindful of us: he will bless us; he will bless the house of Israel; he will bless the house of Aaron. He will bless them that fear the Lord, both small and great. The Lord will increase you more and more, you and your children. Ye are blessed of the Lord which made heaven and earth."

Most Christians don't know what God thinks about them. Through studying the Word of God, I have learned that God thinks good thoughts towards his children.

Jeremiah 29:11 says, "I know the thoughts that I think towards you, saith the Lord, thoughts of peace, and not of evil, to give you an expected end."

Jeremiah 29:11 (Spirit Filled Life Bible) says, "For I know the thoughts that I think towards you, says the Lord, thoughts of peace and not of evil, to give you a future and a hope."

Isaiah 55:8,9 says, "For my thoughts are not your thoughts, neither are your ways my ways, saith the Lord. For as the heavens are higher than the earth, so are my ways higher than your ways, and my thoughts than your thoughts."

The way we see ourselves is not the way God sees us. The way we think about ourselves is not the way God thinks about us. God's ways are higher than our ways and his thoughts are higher than our thoughts.

If God thinks good thoughts towards us, how much more should we think good thoughts towards ourselves.

What kind of thoughts have you been thinking? Are they thoughts of peace or thoughts of evil? You must decide how you are going to think. The choice is up to you. You Can Make a Change!